ONE HUNDRED POEMS FROM
THE JAPANESE

BOOKS BY KENNETH REXROTH

POEMS

The Homestead Called Damascus
The Art of Worldly Wisdom
In What Hour
The Phoenix and the Tortoise
The Dragon and the Unicorn
The Signature of All Things
In Defense of the Earth
Thou Shalt Not Kill
A Bestiary
The Collected Shorter Poems
The Collected Longer Poems

PLAYS

Beyond the Mountains

EDITOR

Selected Poems of D. H. Lawrence
New British Poets

TRANSLATIONS

Fourteen Poems of O. V. Lubicz-Milosz
100 Poems from the Japanese
100 Poems from the Chinese
100 French Poems
Poems from the Greek Anthology
30 Spanish Poems of Love and Exile
Selected Poems of Pierre Reverdy

ESSAYS

Bird in the Bush
Assays

An Autobiographical Novel

ONE HUNDRED POEMS
FROM THE JAPANESE

by

KENNETH REXROTH

A NEW DIRECTIONS BOOK

SIXTH PRINTING

TABLE OF CONTENTS

FOR MARTHE

Murasaki:
    The troubled waters
    Are frozen fast.
    Under clear heaven
    Moonlight and shadow
    Ebb and flow.

Genji:
    The memories of long love
    Gather like drifting snow,
    Poignant as the mandarin ducks,
    Who float side by side in sleep.

INTRODUCTION

It is common to stress the many ways in which Japanese poetry differs from English or Western European, or, for that matter, all other verse. Great as these differences are, and they are profound, the Japanese still wrote poetry. Japanese poetry does what poetry does everywhere: it intensifies and exalts experience. It is true that it concentrates practically exclusively on this function. The poetry of other peoples usually serves other functions too, some of them not particularly germane to the poetic experience. It is possible to claim that Japanese poetry is purer, more essentially poetic. Certainly it is less distracted by non-poetic considerations.

Many, especially Japanese, editors and translators have been embarrassed by this intensity and concentration and have labored to explain each poem until it has been explained away. Often the explanation has obtruded into the poem itself, which has been expanded with concealed commentary and interpretation. Often the translator has simply expanded the poem, relaxed its concentration, usually into platitude. This is all too easy to do, because Japanese poetry depends first of all on the subtlety of its effects. It is a poetry of sensibility. If these effects are extended and diluted, the sensibility easily degenerates into sentimentality.

There are of course manifest differences from Western poetry. One is apparent at a glance. Japanese poems are much shorter, shorter than all but a few poems which consist of a quatrain, couplet, or elegiac distich only. Until modern times the largest body of Western poetry like them was in the *Greek Anthology*. And it is in the *Anthology*, in the poems of a few writers, especially Anyte of Tegea, that the special kind of sensibility cultivated by the Japanese is to be found as the exclusive preoccupation of the poet.

A poetry of sensibility no longer seems as strange as it did to the first translators. Mallarmé, the early Rilke, Emily Dickinson, various others, deal with experience in similar terms. Also, there is a large body of verse directly influenced by Japanese, and there are the fine translations of Arthur Waley.

In my own translations I have tried to interfere as little as possible with the simplicity of the Japanese text. I have always striven for maximum compression. Some of my versions manage with considerably fewer syllables than the originals. On the other hand, I have not sacrificed certain Japanese ornaments which some have considered nonsense or decorative excrescences.

None of the poems is of a character to require an extensive apparatus of notes. They do not deal with experiences special to the Japanese. If they echo other poems, or make use of references unknown to Western readers, this is not essential to an appreciation of the poems. As a matter of fact, in the best periods literary and historical allusion is much less common in Japanese than in Chinese poetry.

I should like the poems in this collection to stand as poetry in English, and even, in a sense, as poetry by a contemporary American poet, because I have chosen only those poems with which I felt considerable identification. On the whole, they are as literal as any versions I know except Waley's. Nonetheless, the putting of them into English has been a creative process, differing only in power from that with which I would express my own thoughts.

The earliest surviving Japanese poetry is in the two mythical and semi-mythical chronicles, the *Kojiki* and the *Nihon Shoki* (*Nihonji*). It is not unlike other primitive poetry. Many of the poems were probably folksongs. Many of them are erotic. They can best be understood by comparison with the songs of the Chinese *Shi Ching*, especially as that collection is interpreted by Marcel Granet in *Festivals and Songs of Ancient China*. They are commonly spoken of as almost devoid of literary value, a judgment with which I do not concur.

With the introduction of writing, in Chinese characters, probably early in the fifth century, Japanese poetry seems already to have assumed the form it was going to keep for over a thousand years. The oldest and most important anthology, the *Manyōshū*, which was compiled in the middle of the eighth century, has nothing primitive about it. If there are any archaic echoes, they are as likely to be from the *Shi Ching* as from the songs of pre-civilized Japan. Later Japanese poetry will show considerable Chinese influence, especially of Po Chu-I, who became a sort of deity of poetry in Japan. The poetry of the *Manyōshū* is courtly, highly sophisticated, formally restricted, and, compared with Western verse, somewhat restricted in subject matter. Most of the accepted themes — autumn leaves, falling snow, plum and cherry blossoms, the moon in its phases and seasons, the rustle of leaves, the songs of cicadas, crickets, frogs, cuckoos, and the *uguisu* (called by some translators a nightingale), assignations with clandestine lovers, famous beauty spots, court ceremonies, the quiet of the monk's hermitage, the death of rulers, patrons and mistresses, and the poem written by the poet on the eve of his own death — the whole repertory of classical Japanese poetry appears at once. The principal changes will take place, not in subject matter, but in quality of sentiment. Later centuries will show the influence of Shingon Buddhist sacramentalism, Zen mysticism, Amidist piety, and finally, the middle class sentiment of the Yedo period.

Curiously enough, there is less apparent influence of the Chinese than might be expected. There is a vast quantity of Chinese poetry written by Japanese and it seems to have absorbed most such tendencies. It happens that with very few exceptions — Murasaki and Sei Shonagon are possibly two — the ability to write in Chinese was confined to men. Poetry in Japanese was written in the Japanese syllabaries. These, however, were not introduced until the ninth century. Prior to that time it is possible that the poems of the *Manyōshū* were more current orally, and the written text, which is in a barbarous, and today not completely intelligible, adaptation of Chinese characters to partly phonetic use, called *Manyogana*, was kept only as a mnemonic, or at best as a book of reference. Incidentally, few translators mention that poems such as these in this book are still sung. All the more famous ones can be obtained on records. Also, each poem has its characteristic pattern of dance gestures. These are not, however, to be thought of as being as stereotyped as the mudras of India or the ritual gestures of the Shinto priests.

A few poems in the *Manyōshū* are *naga uta*, "long poems." None of these are long by our standards. They are mostly elegies or reveries of moderate length. A few are ballads with archetypal plots found all over the world. Most of the poems are *tanka* of thirty-one syllables arranged 5-7-5-7-7. A few are *sedōka*, "head poems," arranged 5-7-7-5-7-7. Both the *naga uta* and the *sedōka* were soon abandoned. Exclusive of poems in Chinese and folksongs, the latter almost always in lines of seven and five syllables, as in the common *dodoitsu*, 7-7-7-5, the *tanka* became the only form to be used until the development of the *haiku* (*hokku*) of only seventeen syllables. A possible exception are the *rengō*, linked poems, *tanka* in series, popular at poem parties, which sometimes assume the organic unity of a continuous poem.

I am aware that most Japanese do not share my opinion of *haiku*. But I feel that the great period of classical art and literature ended with the Ashikagas. Thereafter something different—more secular and middle class—took its place. A number of the more famous *haiku* are given in an appendix.

Japanese is without stress accent, and as sung or recited as poetry, although not when spoken, has very little quantitative difference of syllables. All syllables are open vowels (in classical Japanese poetry all final nasals are vocalized), there are no true diphthongs, and in the classical language, all consonants are very simple. In terms of sound alone, closest parallels may be Italian, Polynesian, or some Bantu languages. Therefore, the ordinary devices of poetry in English are either impossible (stress accent) or intolerable (regularly repeated rhyme or alliteration). Japanese poets, and probably before them the singers of Japanese folksong, developed a complex and subtle pattern depending mostly on the pitch of the vowels, certain echoes and repetitions which are not the same as rhyme, and a number of peculiar devices of meaning. I know that hitherto Japanese scholars have not paid much attention to vowel pitch, but the singers have. The importance of this factor of vowel pitch is only now beginning to be realized in the poetry of other languages as well except for Chinese, where it has been used consciously for a long time. Some interesting studies have been done in recent years in French, for instance, on the importance of pitch in both speech and prosody, and on the distinct difference in the use of pitch in the speech of men and women, the latter a phenomenon found also in Japanese.

It should be borne in mind that the Japanese language is almost as rich in homonyms and ordinary double meanings as is Chinese. *Engō*, associated words, or words rising from the same concept, occupy a position somewhere between our similes and metaphors and the products of free association in modern verse. To an outlander, most of the Japanese poetic devices could be classed as *engō*; at least, they shade imperceptibly into pillow words.

The pillow word, *makura kotoba*, is a fixed epithet, similar to the Homeric "rosy-fingered dawn," "Ulysses of many devices," "cow-eyed Hera." Fixed epithets are common in primitive poetry all over the world. Many *makura kotoba* seem to have become attached to certain places, things and conditions at a very early period. Later, extensive dictionaries of them were prepared, and in unskilled hands they easily degenerate into monotony. Even Hitomara uses "vine-covered" for his province of Iwami, seemingly only because "vine-covered" is the pillow word for *iwa*, "rock." By the time of the *Manyōshū* the meaning of some of them had become doubtful. An excellent example is *ashibiki*, the pillow word for *yama*, "mountain," which occurs in a poem of Hitomaro's discussed in the notes. No one is really sure that *ashibiki* meant "tiring to the feet." That interpretation simply seemed to later generations a plausible pillow word for "mountain."

In the same poem, the entire opening phrase, "the spreading tail feathers of the pheasant of the mountain tiring to the feet," is a *jōshi*, or preface, and serves to create a setting for the last two lines, "through the long, long night I sleep alone." Very often these prefaces have only an emotional or metaphoric relevance, and introduce into a poem of only thirty-one syllables an element of dissociation much like that found in modern French verse. Hitomaro's poem, one of the most famous in Japanese literature, also illustrates the assonance and repetition of vowels, and the intensive repetition, *naga nagashi yo*, "the long, long night," which are all characteristic features of Japanese prosody.

The first poem in Waley's *The Uta* is even more remarkable prosodically. It goes:

> *Futari yukedo*
> *Yuki sugi gataki*
> *Aki yama wo*
> *Ikade ka kimi ga*
> *Hitori koge namu.*

Note the pattern of the vowels: the first line, u-a-i, u-e-o, all the Japanese vowels; the second, u-i, u-i, a-a-i; the third, a-i, a-a, o; the fourth, i-a-e, a, i-i, a; the fifth, i-o-i, o-e, a-u, all the vowels again. It is difficult to conceive of greater sophistication in simplicity. This poem, from the *Manyōshū*, was written by the Princess Ōku in the seventh century. Of course it can be said that this vowel pitch pattern is purely fortuitous, and due to the small number of vowels in Japanese. But I do not know what the word fortuitous means as applied to poetry; presumably the first western hexameter was also fortuitous. It is very easy to demonstrate the melody of such a pattern by assigning definite pitch to each vowel, rising from o to i, and then singing the poem.

The *kake kotoba* or pivot word is a word or part of a word employed in two senses, or, very rarely, in three, one relating to what precedes, the other to what follows. It is a device not unknown to late Latin and it turns up now and then in English humor and frequently in James Joyce's *Finnegans Wake*. The word *matsu*, for example, is often used in the sense of "pine" and "long for" exactly as in the English "pine" and "pine." *Naku* is used in the double sense of "cry" and "without." Thus, "For you I pine of Mount Inaba (if I go away) more steadfast than the ivy covered rock." Or, "Under the waning Autumn moon, the cuckoo cries-outside our honeymoon cottage in the mountains." The poem of Minamoto no Toru in this collection, and the poems about Naniwa are full of possible pivot words and double meanings. It would be impossible to reproduce most pivot words, as pivot words, without barbarism, although, as I recall, Victor Dickins attempted it.

The pivot word shades into the pun, and some Japanese poems have so many puns that they may have two or more quite dissimilar meanings. A good example is the poem of the Stewardess of the Empress Kōka, discussed in the notes.

It would require more than a hundred or so poems to make the history of Japanese classical poetry comprehensible. Briefly, it falls into three periods. The poetry of the *Manyōshū*, compiled in 759 of the Western Era, is characteristically clear, strong and fresh, as might be expected from the first phase of the art. The *Kokinshū*, gathered in 905, in the Heian Period, is a more elegant and subtle collection. Until the reformation of taste in the eighteenth century, it was usually ranked above the *Manyōshū*. *Kokinshū* poetry is more highly stylized and shows the first influences of Buddhist ideas, which are almost totally lacking in the *Manyōshū*. Yet in the *Kokinshū* there is already discernible a certain weakening. The freshness and vigor of the eighth century was going. A definite lassitude and pessimism develops in the poetry of the next period, best represented in the *Shin Kokinshū*. Other characteristics of this, the early Kamakura period, are symbolism, literary reference, and the beginnings of Zenist mysticism. After the middle of the Kamakura epoch, I feel that Japanese *tanka* slowly deteriorated, to be replaced in popularity by *haiku* in the seventeenth and eighteenth centuries.

The poems in this collection are mostly from the *Manyōshū*, the *Kokinshū*, and the curious anthology, the *Hyakunin Isshū*, "Single Poems of a Hundred Poets." The latter is a very uneven collection. It contains some of the most mannered poetry of classical Japan, but it also contains some of the best. I used it because it was readily available. There have been many translations of the *Hyakunin Isshū*, there are innumerable Japanese editions of it, and it is also the basis of a very popular card game. A few poems come from elsewhere, and several are reworkings of poems available to me only in Waley's collection.

The *romaji* texts in this volume come from many sources, including, in some cases, my own transliterations. Rather than make any rash conjectures, I have tended to leave them intact as I found them, except where they seemed patently wrong or out of date. After considerable thought, I have eliminated the hyphenation which was once so commonly used in transliterating Japanese. It is never consistent. Readers of Japanese do not need it. For those who want the Japanese text only to try to capture some of the music of the verse, the hyphens are a distraction. I have also vocalized final nasals, that is, written *"mu"* where the modern language has *"n"*, wherever, which is almost always, this is essential to the verse pattern.

Classical Japanese poetry is read in a slow drone, usually a low falsetto; that is, the voice is kept lower and more resonant than its normal pitch, with equal time and stress on each syllable. This is quite unlike spoken Japanese. Each vowel, including the "u" in final *"tsu"*, is pronounced, more or less as in Italian. Doubled vowels, "ō" and "ū", are pronounced "o-o" and "u-u."

A few of these translations date back many years, one to my adolescence (it happens to be perfectly literal) so there is a certain amount of inconsistency in degree of literalness. Over the years the relationship to the Japanese poem was always a personal and creative one, and in some cases the mood of the moment led me to develop slightly certain implicits or suppress certain obvious explicits. Hardly ever are there many more syllables in the English poem than in the Japanese original, and in ninety out of a hundred examples the translation is as accurate and brief as I could manage. I have never tried to explain away the poem, to translate the elusive into the obvious, as has been, unfortunately, so often the case with translators from the Japanese in the past — always of course with the great exception of Arthur Waley.

I wish to acknowledge the aid of a Guggenheim Fellowship, which gave me leisure in 1948-49 to work on this book as well as others of my own. I am also greatly in debt to Katue Kitasono, himself a poet and artist and editor of the magazine *Vou*, who read the book in manuscript and made several valuable suggestions, and who also obtained for me the beautiful calligraphy by Ukai Uchiyama.

Like the *Three Hundred Poems of T'ang* and other Far Eastern anthologies, this "Hundred Poems" contains a few more for good measure and good luck.

KENNETH REXROTH

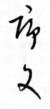

ONE HUNDRED JAPANESE POEMS

I

I passed by the beach
At Tago and saw
The snow falling, pure white,
High on the peak of Fuji.

Tago no ura yu
Uchi idete mireba
Mashiro ni zo
Fuji no takane ni
Yuki wa furikeru

YAMABE NO AKAHITO

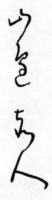

II

When I went out
In the Spring meadows
To gather violets,
I enjoyed myself
So much that I stayed all night.

Haru no nu ni
Sumire tsumi ni to
Koshi ware zo
Nu wo natsukashimi
Hito yo nenikeru

AKAHITO

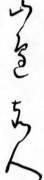

III

Tomorrow I was
Going to the Spring meadows
To pick the young greens.
It snowed all day yesterday
And snowed all day today.

Asu yoriwa
Haruna tsumanuto
Shimeshi nu ni
Kinō mo kyō mo
Yuki wa furi tsutsu

AKAHITO

IV

On Fujiyama
Under the midsummer moon
The snow melts, and falls
Again the same night.

Fuji no ne ni
Furi okeru yuki wa
Mina tzuki no
Mochi ni kenureba
Sono yo furi keri

AKAHITO

V

The mists rise over
The still pools at Asuka.
Memory does not
Pass away so easily.

Asuka gawa
Kawa yodo sarazu
Tatsu kiri no
Omoi sugu beki
Koi ni aranaku ni

AKAHITO

VI

I wish I were close
To you as the wet skirt of
A salt girl to her body.
I think of you always.

Suma no ama no
Shio yaki ginu no
Narenaba ka
Hito hi mo kimi wo
Wasurete omowamu

AKAHITO

VII

I should not have waited.
It would have been better
To have slept and dreamed,
Than to have watched night pass,
And this slow moon sink.

Yasura wa de
Ne na mashi mono wo
Sayo fukete
Katabuku made no
Tsuki wo mishi kana

LADY AKAZOME EMON

VIII

Though the purity
Of the moonlight has silenced
Both nightingale and
Cricket, the cuckoo alone
Sings all the white night.

Uguisu mo
Korogi mo ne wo
Uchitae te
Sayakeki yoru wo
Naku hototogisu

ANONYMOUS

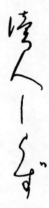

IX

The purity of the moonlight,
Falling out of the immense sky,
Is so great that it freezes
The water touched by its rays.

Ō zora no
Tsuki no hikari shi
Kiyokereba
Kage mishi mizu zo
Mazu kōri keru

ANONYMOUS

X

The cicada sings
In the rotten willow.
Antares, the fire star,
Rolls in the west.

Kare yanagi
Semi shigure shite
Nishizora wa
Akaboshi hitotsu
Hikari sometaru

ANONYMOUS

XI

In a gust of wind the white dew
On the Autumn grass
Scatters like a broken necklace.

Shira tsuyu ni
Kaze no fukishiku
Aki no no wa
Tsuranuki tomenu
Tama zo chirikeru

BUNYA NO ASAYASU

XII

I think of the days
Before I met her
When I seemed to have
No troubles at all.

Ai mite no
Nochi no kokoro ni
Kurabureba
Mukashi wa mono wo
Omowazarikeri

FUJIWARA NO ATSUTADA

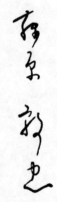

XIII

As I watch the moon
Shining on pain's myriad paths,
I know I am not
Alone involved in Autumn.

Tsuki mireba
Chiji ni mono koso
Kanashi kere
Waga mi hitotsu no
Aki ni wa aranedo

ŌE NO CHISATO

XIV

Autumn has come
To the lonely cottage,
Buried in dense hop vines,
Which no one visits.

Yae mugura
Shigereru yado no
Sabishiki ni
Hito koso miene
Aki wa ki ni keri

THE MONK EIKEI

XV

If the winds of heaven
Would only blow shut the doors
Of the corridors
Of the clouds, I could
Keep these beautiful girls
For a little while.

Amatsu kaze
Kumo no kayoiji
Fuki toji yo
Otome no sugata
Shibashi todomenu

THE ABBOT HENJŌ

XVI

The pheasant of the mountain,
Tiring to the feet,
Spreads his tail feathers.
Through the long, long night
I sleep alone.

Ashibiki no
Yamadori no o no
Shidari o no
Naga nagashi yo wo
Hitori ka mo nemu

KAKINOMOTO NO HITOMARO

XVII

In the empty mountains
The leaves of the bamboo grass
Rustle in the wind.
I think of a girl
Who is not here.

Sasa no ha wa
Miyama mo saya ni
Sayagedomo
Ware wa imo omō
Wakare kinureba

HITOMARO

XVIII

In the Autumn mountains
The colored leaves are falling.
If I could hold them back,
I could still see her.

Aki yama ni
Otsuru momiji ba
Shimashiku wa
Na chiri midare so
Imo ga atari minu

HITOMARO

XIX

Gossip grows like weeds
In a summer meadow.
My girl and I
Sleep arm in arm.

Hito goto wa
Natsu no no kusa to
Shigeku to mo
Imo to ware to shi
Tazusawarineba

HITOMARO

XX

This morning I will not
Comb my hair.
It has lain
Pillowed on the hand of my lover.

Asa ne gami
Ware wa kezuraji
Utsukushiki
Kimi ga ta makura
Fureteshi mono wo

HITOMARO

XXI

Your hair has turned white
While your heart stayed
Knotted against me.
I shall never
Loosen it now.

Kuro kami no
Shira kami made to
Musubiteshi
Kokoro hitotsu wo
Ima takame ya mo

HITOMARO

XXII

A strange old man
Stops me,
Looking out of my deep mirror.

Masu kagami
Soko naru kage ni
Mukai ite miru
Toki ni koso
Shiranu okina ni
Au kokochi sure

HITOMARO

XXIII

The colored leaves
Have hidden the paths
On the autumn mountain.
How can I find my girl,
Wandering on ways I do not know?

Aki yama no
Momiji wo shigemi
Mado inuru
Imo wo motomenu
Yama ji shirazu mo

HITOMARO

XXIV

When I left my girl
In her grave on Mount Hikite
And walked down the mountain path,
I felt as though I were dead.

Fusuma ji wo
Hikite no yama ni
Imo wo okite
Yama ji wo yukeba
Ikeri to mo nashi

HITOMARO

XXV

I sit at home
In our room
By our bed
Gazing at your pillow.

Ie ni kite
Waga ya wo mireba
Tama doko no
Hoka ni mukikeri
Imo ga ko makura

HITOMARO

XXVI

May those who are born after me
Never travel such roads of love.

Ware yu nochi
Umaremu hito wa
Waga gotoku
Koi suru michi ni
Ai kosu na yume

HITOMARO

XXVII

My girl is waiting for me
And does not know
That my body will stay here
On the rocks of Mount Kamo.

Kamo yama no
Iwane shi makeru
Ware wo kamo
Shira ni to imo ga
Machitsutsu aramu

HITOMARO

XXVIII

On the shingle
Beaten by waves
He sleeps with his head
Amongst the rocks.

Oki tsunami
Ki yoru ariso wo
Shikitae no
Makura to makite
Naseru kimi kamo

HITOMARO

XXIX

I waited for my
Lover until I could hear
In the night the oars of the boat
Crossing the River of Heaven.

Waga seko ni
Urakoi oreba
Ama no gawa
Yobune kogi toyomu
Kaji no to kikoyu

HITOMARO?

XXX

Will he always love me?
I cannot read his heart.
This morning my thoughts
Are as disordered
As my black hair.

Nagakaramu
Kokoro mo shirazu
Kurokami no
Midarete kesa wa
Mono wo koso omoe

LADY HORIKAWA

XXXI

Is it your command
That we must pass through this life
Not meeting, even
For a space short as the nodes
Of the reeds of Naniwa?

Naniwa gata
Mijikaki ashi no
Fushi no ma mo
Awade kono yo wo
Sugushite yo to ya

LADY ISE

XXXII

Will I cease to be,
Or will I remember
Beyond the world,
Our last meeting together?

Arazaramu
Kono yo no hoka no
Omoide ni
Ima hito tabi no
Au koto mogana

LADY IZUMI SHIKIBU

XXXIII

I go out of the darkness
Onto a road of darkness
Lit only by the far off
Moon on the edge of the mountains.

Kuraki yori
Kuraki michi ni zo
Irinu beki
Haruka ni terase
Yama no hi no tsuki

IZUMI

XXXIV

The hanging raindrops
Have not dried from the needles
Of the fir forest
Before the evening mist
Of Autumn rises.

Murasame no
Tsuyu mo mada hinu
Maki no ha ni
Kiri tachi noboru
Aki no yugure

THE MONK JAKUREN

XXXV

Guardian of the gate
Of Suma, how many nights
Have you awakened
At the crying of the shore birds
Of the Isle of Awaji?

Awaji shima
Kayou chidori no
Naku koe ni
Iku yo nezamenu
Suma no sekimori

MINAMOTO NO KANEMASA

XXXVI

Although I hide it
My love shows in my face
So plainly that he asks me,
"Are you thinking of something?"

Shinoburedo
Iro ni ide ni keri
Waga koi wa
Mono ya omou to
Hito no tou made

TAIRA NO KANEMORI

XXXVII

The River Izumi
Floods the plain of Mika.
Did I ever meet her?
Why do I long for her?

Mika no hara
Wakite nagaruru
Izumi gawa
Itsu miki tote ka
Koishikaruramu

FUJIWARA NO GO-KANESUKE

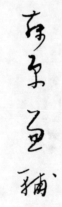

XXXVIII

I dreamed I held
A sword against my flesh.
What does it mean?
It means I shall see you soon.

Tsurugi tachi
Mi ni tori sou to
Ime ni mitsu
Nani no satoshi zomo
Kimi ni awamu tame

LADY KASA

XXXIX

I love and fear him
Steadily as the surf
Roars on the coast at Ise.

Ise no umi no
Iso mo todoro ni
Yosuru nami
Kashikoki hito ni
Koi wataru kamo

LADY KASA

XL

The flowers whirl away
In the wind like snow.
The thing that falls away
Is myself.

Hana sasou
Arashi no niwa no
Yuki narade
Furi yuki mono wa
Waga mi narikeri

THE PRIME MINISTER KINTSUNE

XLI

I may live on until
I long for this time
In which I am so unhappy,
And remember it fondly.

Nagaraeba
Mata kono goro ya
Shinobaremu
Ushi to mishi yo zo
Ima wa koishiki

FUJIWARA NO KIYOSUKE

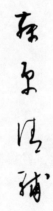

XLII

When I went out in
The Spring fields to pick
The young greens for you
Snow fell on my sleeves.

Kimi ga tame
Haru no no ni idete
Waka na tsumu
Waga koromode ni
Yuki wa furi tsutsu

THE EMPEROR KŌKŌ

XLIII

As certain as color
Passes from the petal,
Irrevocable as flesh,
The gazing eye falls through the world.

Hana no iro wa
Utsuri ni keri na
Itazura ni
Waga mi yo ni furu
Nagame seshi ma ni

THE POETESS ONO NO KOMACHI

XLIV

Imperceptible
It withers in the world,
This flower-like human heart.

Iro miyede
Utsurō mono wa
Yo no naka no
Hito no kokoro no
Hana ni zo arikeru

KOMACHI

XLV

The cricket cries
In the frost.
On my narrow bed,
In a folded quilt,
I sleep alone.

Kirigirisu
Naku ya shimo yo no
Sumu shiro ni
Koromo katashiki
Hitori ka mo nemu

THE REGENT
FUJIWARA NO GO-KYŌGOKU

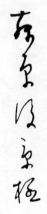

XLVI

From Yoshino
Mountain the autumn
Wind blows. Night wanes.
The village grows cold.
Fullers' mallets sound.

Miyoshino no
Yama no aki kaze
Sayo fukete
Furusato samuku
Koromo utsunari

FUJIWARA NO MASATSUNE

XLVII

In the dawn, although I know
It will grow dark again,
How I hate the coming day.

Akenureba
Kururu mono to wa
Shiri nagara
Nao urameshiki
Asaborake kana

FUJIWARA NO MICHINOBU

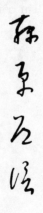

XLVIII

Have you any idea
How long a night can last, spent
Lying alone and sobbing?

Nageki tsutsu
Hitori nuru yo no
Akuru ma wa
Ika ni hisashiki
Mono to ka wa shiru

THE MOTHER
OF THE COMMANDER MICHITSUNA

XLIX

The white chrysanthemum
Is disguised by the first frost.
If I wanted to pick one
I could find it only by chance.

Kokoro ate ni
Orabaya oramu
Hatsu shimo no
Oki madowaseru
Shira giku no hana

ŌSHIKOCHI NO MITSUNE

L

In the mountain village
The wind rustles the leaves.
Deep in the night, the deer
Cry out beyond the edge of dreams.

Yama zato no
Inaba no kaze ni
Nezame shite
Yo fukaku shika no
Koe wo kiku kana

MINAMOTO NO MOROTADA

LI

Your fine promises
Were like the dew of life
To a parched plant,
But now the autumn
Of another year goes by.

Chigiri okishi
Sasemo ga tsuyu wo
Inochi nite
Aware kotoshi no
Aki mo inumeri

FUJIWARA NO MOTOTOSHI

LII

I am unhappy.
I do not care what happens.
I must see you, even
If it means I shall
Be lost in Naniwa Bay.

Wabi mureba
Ima hata onaji
Naniwa naru
Mi wo tsukushite mo
Awamu to zo omou

PRINCE MOTOYOSHI

LIII

I can feel the loneliness
Grow in my mountain village
When the flowers and the eyes
Of men have both gone away.

Yama zato wa
Fuyu zo sabishisa
Masarikeru
Hito me mo kusa mo
Karenu to omoeba

MINAMOTO NO MUNEYUKI

LIV

Someone passes,
And while I wonder
If it is he,
The midnight moon
Is covered with clouds.

Meguri aite
Mishi ya sore to mo
Wakanu mani
Kumo kakurenishi
Yoha no tsuki kage

LADY MURASAKI SHIKIBU

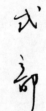

LV

This is not the moon,
Nor is this the spring,
Of other springs,
And I alone
Am still the same.

Tsuki ya aranu
Haru ya mukashi no
Haru naranu
Waga mi hitotsu wa
Moto no mi ni shite

ARIWARA NO NARIHIRA

LVI

I have always known
That at last I would
Take this road, but yesterday
I did not know that it would be today.

Tsui ni yuku
Michi to wa kanete
Kikishi kado
Kinō kyō to wa
Omowazarishi wo

NARIHIRA

LVII

Even in the age
Of the strong swift gods,
I never heard
Of water like Tatsuta River
Dyed with blue and Chinese red.

Chihayaburu
Kami yo mo kikazu
Tatsuta gawa
Kara kurenai ni
Mizu kukuru to wa

NARIHIRA

LVIII

After the storm
On Mount Mimuro,
The colored leaves
Float like brocade
On the River Tatsuta.

*Arashi fuku
Mimuro no yama no
Momiji ba wa
Tatsuta no kawa no
Nishiki narikeri*

THE MONK NŌIN

LIX

As I approach
The mountain village
Through the spring twilight
I hear the sunset bell
Ring through drifting petals.

Yama zato no
Haru no yūgure
Kite mireba
Iriai no kane ni
Hana zo chirikeru

NŌIN

LX

When I am lonely
And go for a walk, I see
Everywhere the same
Autumnal dusk.

Sabishisa ni
Yado wo tachi ide
Nagamureba
Izuku mo onaji
Aki no yūgure

THE MONK RYŌZEN

LXI

You do not come, and I wait
On Matsuo beach,
In the calm of evening.
And like the blazing
Water, I too am burning.

Konu hito wo
Matsuo no ura no
Yūnagi ni
Yaku ya moshio no
Mi mo kogare tsutsu

FUJIWARA NO SADAIE

LXII

As the mists rise in the dawn
From Uji River, one by one,
The stakes of the nets appear,
Stretching far into the shallows.

Asa borake
Uji no kawa giri
Taedae ni
Araware wataru
Seze no ajiro gi

FUJIWARA NO SADAYORI

LXIII

You say, "I will come."
And you do not come.
Now you say, "I will not come."
So I shall expect you.
Have I learned to understand you?

Komu to yū mo
Konu toki aru wo
Koji to yū wo
Komu to wa mataji
Koji to yū mono wo

LADY ŌTOMO NO SAKANOE

LXIV

Do not smile to yourself
Like a green mountain
With a cloud drifting across it.
People will know we are in love.

Aoyama wo
Yoko giru kumo no
Ichijiroku
Ware to emashite
Hito ni shirayu na

SAKANOE

LXV

A cuckoo calls.
When I look there is only
The waning moon
In the early dawn.

Hototogisu
Nakitsuru kata wo
Nagamureba
Tada ariake no
Tsuki zo nokokeru

FUJIWARA NO SANESADA

LXVI

If only the world
Would always remain this way,
Some fishermen
Drawing a little rowboat
Up the river bank.

Yo no naka wa
Tsune ni mogamo na
Nagisa kogu
Ama no obune no
Tsuna de kanashi mo

THE SHŌGUN
MINAMOTO NO SANETOMO

LXVII

Involuntary,
I may live on
In the passing world,
Never forgetting
This midnight moon.

Kokoro ni mo
Arade ukiyo ni
Nagaraeba
Koishikaru beki
Yowa no tsuki kana

THE EMPEROR SANJŌ

LXVIII

Deep in the mountain,
Trampling the red maple leaves,
I hear the stag cry out
In the sorrow of Autumn.

Oku yama ni
Momiji fumi wake
Naku shika no
Koe kiku toki zo
Aki wa kanashiki

THE PRIEST SARUMARU

LXIX

Though you can tell me
You heard a cock crow
In the middle of the night,
The guard at Ōsaka Gate
Will not believe you.

Yo wo komete
Tori no sora ne wa
Hakaru to mo
Yo ni Ōsaka no
Seki wa yurasaji

LADY SEI SHŌNAGON

LXX

All during a night
Of anxiety I wait.
At last the dawn comes
Through the cracks of the shutters,
Heartless as night.

Yo mo sugara
Mono omou koro wa
Ake yarade
Neya no hima sae
Tsure nakarikeri

THE MONK SHUN-E

LXXI

She said she would come
At once, and so I waited
Till the moon rose
In the October dawn.

Ima komu to
Iishi bakari ni
Naga tsuki no
Ari ake no tsuki
Wo machi izuru kana

THE MONK SOSEI

LXXII

For the sake of a night
Short as the nodes
Of the reeds of Naniwa
Must I live on,
My flesh wasted with longing?

Naniwa e no
Ashi no kari ne no
Hito yo yue
Mi wo tsukushite ya
Koi wataru beki

THE STEWARDESS
OF THE EMPRESS KŌKA

LXXIII

That spring night I spent
Pillowed on your arm
Never really happened
Except in a dream.
Unfortunately I am
Talked about anyway.

> *Haru no yo no*
> *Yume bakari naru*
> *Ta makura ni*
> *Kai naku tanamu*
> *Na koso oshikere*

LADY SUO

LXXIV

Yes, I am in love.
They were talking about me
Before daylight,
Although I began to love
Without knowing it.

Koi su tefu
Waga na wa madaki
Tachi ni keri
Hito shirezu koso
Omoi someshi ga

MIBU NO TADAMI

LXXV

As I row over the plain
Of the sea and gaze
Into the distance, the waves
Merge with the bright sky.

Wata no hara
Kagi idete mireba
Hisa kata no
Kumoi ni magō
Okitsu shira nami

FUJIWARA NO TADAMICHI

LXXVI

Since I left her,
Frigid as the setting moon,
There is nothing I loathe
As much as the light
Of dawn on the clouds.

Ari ake no
Tsure naku mieshi
Wakare yori
Aka tsuki bakari
Uki mono wa nashi

MIBU NO TADAMINE

LXXVII

In the eternal
Light of the spring day
The flowers fall away
Like the unquiet heart.

Hisa kata no
Hikari nodokeki
Haru no hi ni
Shizu kokoro naku
Hana no chiruramu

KI NO TOMONORI

LXXVIII

Like Michinoku
Cloth, printed with tangled ferns,
My mind is disordered
Because of you,
But my love is not.

Michinoku no
Shinobu mojizuri
Tare yue ni
Midare somenishi
Ware naranaku ni

MINAMOTO NO TŌRU

LXXIX

In all the world
There is no way whatever.
The stag cries even
In the most remote mountain.

Yo no naka yo
Michi koso nakere
Omoi iru
Yama no oku ni mo
Shika zo nakunaru

THE PRIEST
FUJIWARA NO TOSHINARI

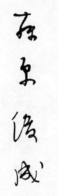

LXXX

In the Bay of Sumi
The waves crowd on the beach.
Even in the night
By the corridors of dreams,
I come to you secretly.

*Sumi no e no
Kishi ni yoru nami
Yoru sae ya
Yume no kayoi ji
Hito me yokuramu*

FUJIWARA NO TOSHIYUKI

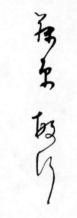

LXXXI

Autumn has come invisibly.
Only the wind's voice is ominous.

> *Aki kinu to*
> *Me ni wa sayaka ni*
> *Miene domo*
> *Kaze no oto ni zo*
> *Odorokarenuru*

TOSHIYUKI

LXXXII

In the evening
The rice leaves in the garden
Rustle in the autumn wind
That blows through my reed hut.

Yū sareba
Kado ta no inaba
Oto zurete
Ashi no maro ya ni
Aki kaze zo fuku

MINAMOTO NO TSUNENOBU

LXXXIII

The wind has stopped
The current of the mountain stream
With only a windrow
Of red maple leaves.

Yama gawa ni
Kaze no kaketaru
Shigarami wa
Nagare mo aenu
Momiji nari keri

HARUMICHI NO TSURAKI

LXXXIV

Out in the marsh reeds
A bird cries out in sorrow,
As though it had recalled
Something better forgotten.

Wasurete mo
Aru beki mono wo
Ashi hara ni
Omoi izuru no
Naku zo kanashiki

KI NO TSURAYUKI

LXXXV

No, the human heart
Is unknowable.
But in my birthplace
The flowers still smell
The same as always.

Hito wa isa
Kokoro mo shirazu
Furusato wa
Hana zo mukashi no
Ka ni nioikeru

TSURAYUKI

LXXXVI

Like a wave crest
Escaped and frozen,
One white egret
Guards the harbor mouth.

Ashi tazu no
Tateru kawa be wo
Fuku kaze ni
Yosete kaeramu
Nami ka to zo omou

THE EMPEROR UDA

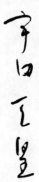

LXXXVII

It does not matter
That I am forgotten,
But I pity
His foresworn life.

Wasuraruru
Mi wo ba omowazu
Chikaikeshi
Hito no inochi no
Oshiku mo aru kana

LADY UKON

LXXXVIII

I will come to you
Through the ford at Saho,
The plovers piping about me
As my horse wades
The clear water.

Chidori naku
Saho no kawa to no
Kiyoki se wo
Uma uchi watashi
Itsu ka kayowamu

ŌTOMO NO YAKAMOCHI

LXXXIX

When I see the first
New moon, faint in the twilight,
I think of the moth eyebrows
Of a girl I saw only once.

Furi sakete
Mika zuki mireba
Hito me mishi
Hito no mayo biki
Omōyuru kamo

YAKAMOCHI

XC

The cry of the stag
Is so loud in the empty
Mountains that an echo
Answers him as though
It were a doe.

Yama biko no
Ai to yomu made
Tsuma goi ni
Ka naku yama be ni
Hitori nomi shite

YAKAMOCHI

XCI

I send you a box
Of glowing pearls.
Wear them with irises
And orange blossoms.

Shira tama wo
Tsutsumite yaraba
Ayame gusa
Hana tachi bana ni
Ae mo nuku gane

YAKAMOCHI

XCII

In the spring garden
Where the peach blossoms
Light the path beneath,
A girl is walking.

Haru no sono
Kurenai niou
Momo no hana
Shita teru michi ni
Ide tatsu otome

YAKAMOCHI

XCIII

I lie long abed
In the morning and listen
To the rivermen
Rowing on the Izumi River.

Asa doko ni
Kikeba harukeshi
Izumi gawa
Asa kogi shitsutsu
Utau funa bito

YAKAMOCHI

XCIV

The wind rustles the bamboos
By my window in the dusk.

Waga yado no
Isasa muratake
Fuku kaze no
Oto no kasokeki
Kono yūbe kamo

YAKAMOCHI

XCV

Mist floats on the Spring meadow.
My heart is lonely.
A nightingale sings in the dusk.

Haru no nu ni
Kasumi tanabiki
Ura ganashi
Kono yū kage ni
Uguisu naku mo

YAKAMOCHI

XCVI

The frost lies white
On the suspended
Magpies' Bridge.
The night is far gone.

Kasasagi no
Wataseru hashi ni
Oku shimo no
Shiroki wo mireba
Yo zo fukenikeru

YAKAMOCHI

XCVII

Now to meet only in dreams,
Bitterly seeking,
Starting from sleep,
Groping in the dark
With hands that touch nothing.

Ime no ai wa
Kurushikarikeri
Odorokite
Kaki saguredomo
Te ni mo fureneba

YAKAMOCHI

XCVIII

We were together
Only a little while,
And we believed our love
Would last a thousand years.

Kaku shi nomi
Arikeru mono wo
Imo mo ware mo
Chi tose no gotoku
Tanomitarikeru

YAKAMOCHI

XCIX

Others may forget you, but not I.
I am haunted by your beautiful ghost.

Hito wa isa
Omoi yamu tomo
Tama kazura
Kage ni mie tsutsu
Wasuraenu ka mo

THE EMPRESS YAMATOHIME

C

The deer on pine mountain,
Where there are no falling leaves,
Knows the coming of autumn
Only by the sound of his own voice.

Momiji senu
Tokiwa no yama ni
Sumu shika wa
Onore nakite ya
Aki wo shiruramu

ŌNAKATOMI NO YOSHINOBU

CI

Falling from the ridge
Of high Tsukuba,
The Minano River
At last gathers itself,
Like my love, into
A deep, still pool.

Tsukuba ne no
Mine yori otsuru
Minano gawa
Koi zo tsumorite
Fuchi to narikeru

THE EMPEROR YŌZEI

CII

I must leave you, but
If I hear the sound
Of the pine that grows
On Mount Inaba,
I shall come back at once.

Tachi wakare
Inaba no yama no
Mine ni ouru
Matsu to shi kikaba
Ima kaeri komu

ARIWARA NO YUKIHIRA

THREE NAGA UTA *from* HITOMARO
CIII

In the sea of ivy clothed Iwami
Near the cape of Kara,
The deep sea miru weed
Grows on the sunken reefs;
The jewelled sea tangle
Grows on the rocky foreshore.
Swaying like the jewelled sea tangle
My girl would lie with me,
My girl whom I love with a love
Deep as the miru growing ocean.
We slept together only a few

> *Tsunusa hau*
> *Iwami no umi no*
> *Koto saegu*
> *Kara no saki naru*
> *Ikuri ni zo*
> *Fuka miru ouru*
> *Ariso ni zo*
> *Tama mo wa ouru*
> *Tama mo nasu*
> *Nabiki neshi ko wo*
> *Fuka miru no*
> *Fukamete moedo*
> *Sa neshi yo wa*
> *Ikuda mo arazu*
> *Hau tsuta no*
> *Wakare shi kureba*

Wonderful nights and then
I had to leave her.
It was like tearing apart braided vines.
My bowels are knotted inside me
With the pain of my heart.
I long for her and look back.
A confusion of colored leaves
Falls over Mount Watari.
I can no longer see
Her waving sleeves.
The moon rushes through rifted clouds
Over the honeymoon cottage

Kimo mukau
Kokoro wo itami
Omoi tsutsu
Kaerimi suredo
Ō bune no
Watari no yama no
Momiji ba no
Chiri no midari ni
Imo ga sode
Saya ni mo miezu
Tsuma gomoru
Yagami no yama no
Kumo ma yori
Watarau tsuki no
Oshikedomo

On Mount Yagami.
The setting sun has left the sky.
The light grows dim.
I thought I was a brave man.
My thin sleeves are wet with tears.

Kakuroi kureba
Ama zutau
Iri hi sashinure
Masurao to
Omoeru ware mo
Shikitae no
Koromo no sode wa
Tōrite nurenu

HITOMARO

CIV

The Bay of Tsunu
In the sea of Iwami
Has no fine beaches
And is not considered beautiful.
Perhaps it is not,
But we used to walk
By the sea of the whale fishers
Over the rocky shingle of Watazu
Where the wind blows
The green jewelled seaweed
Like wings quivering in the morning,

Iwami no umi
Tsunu no urami wo
Ura nashi to
Hito koso mirame
Kata nashi to
Hito koso mirame
Yoshieyashi
Ura wa naku to mo
Yoshieyashi
Kata wa naku to mo
Isana tori
Umibe wo sashite
Watazu no
Ariso no ue ni
Ka ao naru
Tama mo okitsu mo

And the waves rock the kelp beds
Like wings quivering in the evening.
Just as the sea tangle sways and floats
At one with the waves,
So my girl clung to me
As she lay by my side.
Now I have left her,
To fade like the hoarfrost.
I looked back ten thousand times
At every turn of the road.
Our village fell away,
Farther and farther away.
The mountains rose between us,

Asa ha furu
Kaze koso yoseme
Yū ha furu
Nami koso kiyose
Nami no muta
Ka yori kaku yori
Tama mo nasu
Yori neshi imo wo
Tsuyu jimo no
Okite shi kureba
Kono michi no
Yaso kuma goto ni
Yorozu tabi
Kaeri mi suredo

Steeper and steeper.
I know she thinks of me, far off,
And wilts with longing, like summer grass.
Maybe if the mountains would bow down
I could see her again,
Standing in our doorway.

Iya tō ni
Sato wa sakarinu
Iya taka ni
Yama mo koe kinu
Natsu kusa no
Omoi shinaete
Shinuburamu
Imo ga kado mimu
Nabike kono yama

HITOMARO

CV

When she was still alive
We would go out, arm in arm,
And look at the elm trees
Growing on the embankment
In front of our house.
Their branches were interlaced.
Their crowns were dense with spring leaves.
They were like our love.
Love and trust were not enough to turn back
The wheels of life and death.
She faded like a mirage over the desert.

Utsusemi to
Omoishi toki ni
Torimochite
Waga futari mishi
Hashiri de no
Tsutsumi ni tateru
Tsuki no ki no
Kochi gochi no e no
Haru no ha no
Shigeki ga gotoku
Omoerishi
Imo ni wa aredo
Tanomerishi
Kora ni wa aredo
Yo no naka wo
Somukishi eneba

One morning like a bird she was gone
In the white scarves of death.
Now when the child
Whom she left in her memory
Cries and begs for her,
All I can do is pick him up
And hug him clumsily.
I have nothing to give him.
In our bedroom our pillows
Still lie side by side,
As we lay once.

Kagiroi no
Moyuru aranu ni
Shiro tae no
Ama hire gakuri
Tori jimono
Asa tachi imashite
Iri hi nasu
Kakurinishikaba
Wagi moko ga
Kata mi ni okeru
Wakaki ko no
Koi naku goto ni
Tori atau
Mono shi nakereba
Otoko jimono
Waki basami mochi
Wagi moko to
Futari waga neshi

I sit there by myself
And let the days grow dark.
I lie awake at night, sighing till daylight.
No matter how much I mourn
I shall never see her again.
They tell me her spirit
May haunt Mount Hagai
Under the eagles' wings.
I struggle over the ridges
And climb to the summit.
I know all the time

> *Makura zuku*
> *Tsuma ya no uchi ni*
> *Hiru wa mo*
> *Urasabi kurashi*
> *Yoru wa mo*
> *Iki zuki akashi*
> *Nagekedomo*
> *Semu sube shira ni*
> *Kōredomo*
> *Au yoshi wo nami*
> *Ō tori no*
> *Hagai no yama ni*
> *Waga kōru*
> *Imo wa imasu to*
> *Hito no ieba*
> *Iwa ne sakumite*
> *Nazumi koshi*
> *Yokeku mo zo naki*

That I shall never see her,
Not even so much as a faint quiver in the air.
All my longing, all my love
Will never make any difference.

Utsusemi to
Omoishi imo ga
Tama kagiru
Honoka ni dani mo
Mienu omoeba

HITOMARO

A FEW SAMPLES
OF THE MORE FAMOUS HAIKU

Autumn evening —
A crow on a bare branch.   BASHŌ

A wild sea —
In the distance,
Over Sado,
The Milky Way.   BASHŌ

An old pond —
The sound
Of a diving frog.   BASHŌ

On this road
No one will follow me
In the Autumn evening.   BASHŌ

Summer grass
Where warriors dream.   BASHŌ

A blind child
Guided by his mother,
Admires the cherry blossoms.   KIKAKU

The Autumn cicada
Dies by the side
Of its empty shell.   JŌSŌ

The long, long river
A single line
On the snowy plain.   BONCHŌ

Wild goose, wild goose,
At what age
Did you make your first journey?   ISSA

In my life
As in the twilight,
A bell sounds.
I enjoy the freshness of evening.   ISSA

Over the vast field of mustard flowers
The moon rises in the East,
The sun sets in the West.   BUSON

No one spoke,
The host, the guest,
The white chrysanthemums.   RYŌTA

NOTES

YAMABE NO AKAHITO lived during the reign of the Emperor Shōmu, 734-748 A. D. He is thought to have died in 736. He seems to have been in close personal attendance on the Emperor and to have accompanied him on his progresses through the country. His short poems are considered nearly the equal of Hitomaro's, but the latter's *naga uta*, "long poems," are superior. He is a *kasei*, a deified poet. The point of the first poem is the contrast of white on white, and as such, is typical of the kind of perception prized in Japanese poetry. The next poem is often used, especially in the *dodoitsu* form to mean "I had such a good time in the Yoshiwara, or elsewhere in feminine company, I forgot to come home." It would have had this meaning a thousand years later. In Akahito's time it probably referred to one of the ladies of the palace, or, of course, it could even mean just what it says. Again, the third poem could refer to the sudden realization of old age during a love affair with a young girl. Asuka was a former Imperial Palace site; this poem is a *hanka*, a sort of coda to a *naga uta*, as are several others by Akahito, Yakamochi, and Hitomaro.

AKAZOME EMON lived in the eleventh century, a contemporary of Murasaki, Sei Shōnagon, Izumi Shikibu, and Ise Tayū (the Priestess of Ise) — the most brilliant gathering of women in the world's literature. She was the daughter of the poet Taira no Kanemori and the wife of Ōe no Masahira, and a Lady-in-Waiting to the Empress. Akazome Emon is not a true name in the same sense as a man's name in the classical period. Japanese women did not have proper names but were known by titles, nicknames and sometimes derivatives of a husband or father's name.

ANONYMOUS. The first poem could mean: "The salvation of Buddha (or Amida) has enraptured both the householder and the monk or nun, but the prostitute worships in her own way, all through the night." The bird called nightingale by all translators is *Homochlamys cantans* — the *uguisu*, a bushwarbler, not related to the European nightingale. The cuckoo is *cuculus poliocephalus*, the *hototogisu*, a relative of the European and North American cuckoos. The *hototogisu* usually sings in the twilight. Its cry, as well as the *uguisu's*, is often interpreted by the Japanese as *Hokkekyō*, the name of the *Lotus Sutra*. It is also supposed to be a spirit from Hell, and, again, symbolizes the pleasures of the flesh, courtesans and prostitutes, sacred and profane. The second poem could be interpreted similarly, "The promise of Amida's bliss is so powerful (or the Bodhisattva's vow is so effective) that the ocean of Karma grows still."

BUNYA NO ASAYASU lived about 900 A. D. during the reign of the Emperor Daigo. He is the son of Bunya no Yasuhide, whose poetry I have found untranslatable. Asayasu's poem was written at the request of the Emperor during a garden party and poem-writing contest.

FUJIWARA NO ATSUTADA is believed to have died in 961 A. D. He was a *Chūnagon*, a State Adviser, and the son of the *Udaijin*, the Minister of the Right of the Emperor Daigo. The Fujiwara family, or rather, clan, still extant and powerful today, is one of the most extraordinary which has ever existed. For centuries they have provided Japan with administrators, regents, Shōguns, poets, generals, painters, philosophers, and abbots.

ŌE NO CHISATO is believed to have lived about 825 A. D. Nothing else is known of him, although this poem is one of the most famous in Japanese literature.

THE MONK EIKEI. Nothing is known of Eikei except that he wrote towards the end of the tenth century.

THE ABBOT HENJŌ died in 850 A. D. Before he entered the monastic life, he was named Yoshimune no Munesada. He was related to the Imperial family and was a powerful courtier of the Emperor Nimmyō. The word "*sōjō*" is often translated "bishop." There are neither priests nor bishops in Buddhism, but monks and abbots. In Shintō there are priests and priestesses, but no bishops. The poem refers to a dance at court of the daughters of the nobility, on the Feast of Light when the first fruits are offered to the gods and Emperor in the Autumn. The point is that the girls are really moon maidens, and will return to the moon unless the sky becomes overcast.

KAKINOMOTO NO HITOMARO flourished during the reign of the Emperor Mommu, 697-707 A. D. Nothing else is known of him except what can be gathered from his poems. He was possibly a personal attendant of the Emperor. Presumably he spent his later years in Iwami (where he may have been born) and died there. He is generally considered the leading Japanese poet, and is the only Japanese who ever wrote really great "long poems," *naga uta*, which are not long poems but elegies of moderate length. He is a *kasei*, a deified poet. "Tiring to the feet," *ashibiki*, is a pillow-word, *makura kotoba*, for "mountain," *yama*. This is an archaic word the meaning of which is no longer known, but the majority of commentators derive it from *ashi hiku*, "to drag the foot." Others, however, think it means "thickly forested." "Spreads his tail feathers" is *shidari o*, "the spreading tail feathers," a pillow-word for *dori*, "pheasant." The whole phrase is a *jōshi*, or introductory verse, to *Naga nagashi yo*, "the long, long night." Many translators have considered such devices either excrescences or only euphonically related to the meaning of the poem. I feel, however, that with a little study their emotional significance and their function as suppressed metaphors, in almost all cases, can be disentangled. The poem, "My girl is waiting for me," is Hitomaro's death poem. Poem XXII is a *sedōka*. "The oars of the boat crossing the River of Heaven" refers to the seventh night of the seventh month, on which the Herd Boy, Altair, crosses the Milky Way to visit the Weaving Girl, Vega, from whom he is separated all the rest of the year. It is usually said that the magpies link their wings and form a bridge by which the lovers can cross, but sometimes they use a boat. Hitomaro seems to have had at least two "wives," Kibitsu Uneme, who died before him, and another, Yosami, who wrote some poems on his death, as well as the Iwami girl of the *naga utas*.

LADY HORIKAWA is known only as the *Mon in*, attendant, of the Empress Dowager Taiken, in the middle of the twelfth century.

119

LADY ISE was mistress of the Emperor Uda, 888-897, and bore him a son, Prince Katsura. Her father was Fujiwara no Tsugukage, Governor of Ise, from which she came by her name. She was famous for her scholarship and the sweetness of her personality. She is not to be confused with Ise Tayū the Priestess of the Ise shrine in the eleventh century.

Virgins of Ise, for information of readers of *Genji*, were only ritually "pure." The poem contains two quite different meanings which I have tried to combine.

LADY IZUMI SHIKIBU lived at the end of the tenth and the beginning of the eleventh century, a contemporary of Akazome, Murasaki, Sei Shōnagon, and Ise Tayū. She was the daughter of Ōe no Masamune, and the wife of Tachibana no Michisada, the Lord of Izumi, the mistress of Prince Tametaka and his brother Prince Atsumichi, the wife of Fujiwara no Yasumasa, Lord of Tango. Her correspondence with her lover (except the verse, possibly apocryphal) the *Izumi Shikibu Monogatari*, is a masterpiece of Japanese prose. Of all the poets of the classical period, she has, to my mind, the deepest and most poignant Buddhist sensibility.

THE MONK JAKUREN was a Fujiwara; Jakuren is his monastic name. He lived at the end of the twelfth century.

MINAMOTO NO KANEMASA flourished early in the twelfth century. He was a member of another great noble house of Japan, the rivals of the Taira. The word translated "shore birds" is *chidori*, which means sandpipers, plovers, birds like our killdeer and phalaropes. It also means, and is written with the characters for, "the thousand birds." This is my favorite Japanese poem. There is a parallel implied with the guardians of the gates of life, weary with the cries of souls migrating from life to life, and some, passing to the Bliss of Amida's Paradise, or to Nirvana. The meaning "never finding" is implicit in *awaji*; also, *awa* means "spindrift" or "a bubble." This poem is often echoed in later literature, notably by the great erotic novelist Saikaku in his *Futokoro Suzuri*: "Hearing the cries of the shorebirds of the Isle of Awaji, I know the sadness of the worlds." Genji was banished to Suma, and Yukihira, the brother of Narihira; and there the Taira clan, fleeing from the capital with the infant emperor, camped and were surprised and almost exterminated by the Minamoto in a great battle that brought to an end the finest years of Japanese civilization. See also the twenty-six syllable folksongs in Georges Bonneau, *L'expression Poétique dans le Folk-lore Japonais*, Vol. I, pp. 51, 56, 57. (See also the note on Yukihira.)

TAIRA NO KANEMORI flourished in the tenth century. Nothing else is known of him. The Tairas were the third great family of Japan.

FUJIWARA NO GO-KANESUKE lived in the tenth century and had office as a State Councillor, Chūnagon. The first two lines of the poem are an excellent example of the use of a seemingly irrelevant preface, *jōshi*, linked to the rest of the poem emotionally and as a suppressed metaphor.

LADY KASA lived in the eighth century, and was a lover of Yakamochi. She was possibly related to the family of Kasa Kanamura, who made a collection of poetry, some of which was included in the Manyōshū, or to the Monk Manzei, whose secular name was Kasamaro, also a poet of the Manyōshū.

THE PRIME MINISTER KINTSUNE (Nyūdo Saki no Dajō Daijin) held office in the early part of the thirteenth century. Later he became a monk, and founded the temple Saionji.

FUJIWARA NO KIYOSUKE died in 1177. He was the son of Fujiwara no Akisuke, also a poet, and was Lord of Nagato, Vice Steward of the ex-Empress, and held the Senior Fourth Court Rank. The *Zoku Shika Shū* anthology, which he compiled at the order of the Emperor Nijō, was unfinished at the latter's death, and so is not ranked as one of the Imperial Anthologies.

THE EMPEROR KŌKŌ reigned from 885 to 887. This poem was written in his youth.

ONO NO KOMACHI lived from 834 to 880. She is the legendary beauty of Japan. She is supposed to have lost her beauty in old age and become a homeless beggar. This may be true, but it is improbable and is most likely derived from her poems, many of which deal with the transitoriness of life and beauty. She was the daughter of Yoshisada, Lord of Dewa. The second poem echoes the curse of Iha Nagahimi in the Nihongi.

FUJIWARA NO GO-KYŌGOKU was regent, *Sesshō*, and Prime Minister, *Dajō Daijin*, at the end of the twelfth century. This poem has been attributed to Yoshitsune; the twelfth century war lord.

FUJIWARA NO MASATSUNE lived from 1170 to 1221. He was a Sangi, a Councillor of State, with the Junior Third Rank, and was one of the compilers of the anthology, *Shin Kokin Shū*. His father was Toshinari (Shunzei), a famous poet. "Fullers' mallets sound" refers to the beating of cloth in cold water, at the stream's edge — one of the conventional signs of Autumn common to both Chinese and Japanese poetry, in Chinese, *"wen han ch'u,"* "hear cold mallet."

FUJIWARA NO MICHINOBU was born in 973. He became a Lieutenant General and showed great promise as a poet, but died at the age of twenty-two.

THE MOTHER OF THE COMMANDER MICHITSUNA (Udaishō Michitsuna no haha) was the wife of the Regent Kaneie, and lived in the latter part of the tenth century. According to legend, she gave this poem to her husband when he came home very late one night, as he habitually did.

OSHIKOCHI NO MITSUNE lived at the beginning of the tenth century. He was one of the compilers of the *Kokin Shū*.

MINAMOTO NO MOROTADA lived in the twelfth century. He was an officer in the Imperial Guard. Another translation might be

> In the mountain village
> I am awakened
> By the wind in the leaves.
> Deep in the night I hear
> The deer cry out.

PRINCE MOTOYOSHI was the son of the Emperor Yōsei, who reigned from 877 to 884. Again an ambiguity hinged on a double meaning of Naniwa, as in the poem by Lady Ise.

MINAMOTO NO MUNEYUKI lived in the tenth century.

LADY MURASAKI SHIKIBU lived from 974 to 1031. She is the greatest figure in Japanese literature, the author of *The Tale of Genji*, one of the world's greatest books, of a diary, and of numerous poems. She was the daughter of Tametoki, Lord of Echigo, the grand-daughter of Fujiwara no Kanesuke, a well-known poet, and the second wife of Fujiwara no Nobutaka. She was a Lady-in-Waiting to the Empress Akiko. Shikibu is a title, actually a military one, which seems to have been given to important women of the court as a courtesy. Murasaki is the name of the wife of Genji in her novel. Arthur Waley gives a complete biography in the introduction to his translation of *Genji*.

ARIWARA NO NARIHIRA lived in the middle of the ninth century. The *Ise Monogatari* purports to be based upon his diaries, but it is more likely a largely fictional romance developed by imagining situations for his poems. He is the legendary great lover of Japanese literature and there are several plays and Noh dramas about him. *Kakitsubata*, translated by Pound, is one of the most subtle and beautiful of all Noh plays. In the poem about Tatsuta River, the reference, is to what we call tie-and-dye. The blue is understood as the ground color of the red. Note the resemblance to Western prosody, especially in the first poem.

THE MONK NŌIN lived in the eleventh century. His secular name was Tachibana no Nagayasu. Compare the second poem with the *haiku* by Issa.

THE MONK RYŌZEN was a monk of the Gion Temple near Kyōto during the eleventh century.

FUJIWARA NO SADAIE lived from 1162 to 1242. He was an Imperial Vice-Councillor, *Gon-Chūnagon*, and the compiler of the *Hyakunin isshu*, "Single Poems by a Hundred Poets," from which over half of the poems in this book are taken.

He assisted in the compilation of the *Shin Kokin Shū* for the retired Emperor Go-Toba and the *Shin Chokusen Shū* for the Emperor Go-Horikawa, and left a diary, the Meigetsu-Ke, or "Bright Moon Diary." The translation is free — the Japanese refers to the "burning" sea water in the salt kilns.

FUJIWARA NO SADAYORI wasa *Gon-Chūnagon*, or Vice Councillor, in the middle of the eleventh century.

LADY ŌTOMO NO SAKANOE lived at the beginning of the eighth century. She was the aunt of Ōtomo Yakamochi. In poem LXIII elide *toyū*.

FUJIWARA NO SANESADA (Go Tokudaiji no Sadaijin) was Minister of the Left of the Temple Tokudaiji at the end of the twelfth century. In the *dodoitsu* form this is one of the most popular geisha songs.

THE SHŌGUN MINAMOTO NO SANEMOTO (Kamakura no Udaijin) was only nominally *Shōgun* and exercised none of the authority of the office, but spent his time in writing, calligraphy, and the appreciation of the arts. In 1219 he was murdered at the shrine of Hachiman, the God of War, in Kamakura, by his nephew, the Priest Kugyō. With his death the Minamoto clan lost all of its power.

THE EMPEROR SANJŌ reigned from 1012 to 1017, when he was forced to retire by the Regent Fujiwara no Michinaga.

THE PRIEST SARUMARU lived before the ninth century. He was a *Tayū*, or priest of a Shintō shrine. Outside of these two facts, only legends are known of him.

LADY SEI SHŌNAGON was born in 967, the daughter of Kiyohara no Motosuke, a descendant of the Emperor Temmu, who was a poet, a teacher of poetry, and one of the compilers of the *Gosen Shū* anthology, as well as Governor of the Province of Bingo. She was an attendant of the Empress Sadako. (Shōnagon is the title of her office.) She is the author of the famous "Pillow Book," *Makura no Sōshi*, a half diary, half book of short essays and *pensées*, a class of literature peculiar to China and Japan, and something like the *Essays* of Montaigne or a very secular *Pensées* of Pascal. She was considerably of a blue stocking, with somewhat of a waspish temper, which the poem given here reflects. My translation is a possible meaning of the poem, but the accepted meaning is too complex to stand translation: Briefly, a Chinese warrior once escaped from captivity when one of his retainers imitated the crowing of a cock so perfectly that the guards lowered the gates of the city in which they were held. Sei says that although the imitation of a cock's crow may fool the world, the guards of Ōsaka Gate (which means "the Gate of the Hill of Meeting") will not permit subterfuge — that is, it is not possible to gain an assignation with her by vulgar devices. Ōsaka is not, of course, the modern city, but a hill East of Kyōto and South of Lake Biwa.

THE MONK SHUN-E lived in the twelfth century. He was the son of Minamoto no Toshiyori, a Senior State Councillor and compiler of the *Kin yō Shū* Anthology.

THE MONK SOSEI, whose lay name was Yoshimine no Hironobu, lived at the end of the ninth century. He was the son of the Abbot Henjō.

THE STEWARDESS OF THE EMPRESS KŌKA (Kōka Mon-in no Bettō) was the daughter of Fujiwara no Toshitaka and lived in the twelfth century. The poem also means, "For the sake of a joint of a reed of Naniwa Bay, shall I wade past the depth-measuring gauge."

THE LADY SUO was the daughter of Taira no Tsugunaka, Governor of Suo, and a Lady-in-Waiting of the Emperor Go-Reizei, who reigned in the middle of the eleventh century. The commentators give several legends, all improbable, about the occasion of the poem.

MIBU NO TADAMI lived in the tenth century.

FUJIWARA NO TADAMICHI was Regent and Prime Minister in the latter part of the twelfth century.

MIBU NO TADAMINE lived in the tenth century. This poem has often been considered the best of the *Kokin Shū*, of which Tadamine was one of the compilers. His dates are sometimes given as 867-965.

KI NO TOMONORI lived in the early tenth century. He was a nephew of Tsurayuki and aided him in compiling the *Kokin Shū*.

MINAMOTO NO TŌRU (Kawara no Sadaijin) died in 949. He was Minister of the Left, *Sadaijin*, living in Kawara, a part of Kyōto. The poem is very elliptical in Japanese; another reading could be:

> Some woman
> Has made my mind as
> Disordered as Michinoku
> Cloth, printed with tangled ferns.
> It did not get that way
> By itself.

THE PRIEST FUJIWARA NO TOSHINARA died in the year 1205. He was a courtier of the Empress Dowager Kogu and later became a Shintō priest. He is also known by the Chinese pronunciation of his name, *Shunzei*, by his priestly name, *Shakua*, and by the title, *Kotai Kogu no tayū Toshinari*. He was poetry instructor of the Emperor Go-Toba and one of the leaders of the poetic renascence of that Monarch's court. He was also a famous painter and calligrapher.

FUJIWARA NO TOSHIYUKI lived from 880 to 907. He was an officer of the Imperial Guard and a famous calligrapher as well as poet. The poem is a good illustration of the use of a seemingly irrelevant preface. The first two lines are linked to the rest of the poem by the word *yoru*, the "crowding" of the waves, which is repeated in the third line in the sense of "night."

MINAMOTO NO TSUNENOBU lived in the latter half of the eleventh century. He was a *Dainagon*, or Minister of State. Implicit in the poem is the notion that the rustling of rice leaves by the hut of the hermit reminds him of the rustle of silk skirts of the court he has abandoned. Tsunenobu himself never became a recluse. He was famous as a poet, painter, calligrapher, and musician.

HARUMICHI NO TSURAKI lived in the first quarter of the tenth century. He was a provincial governor.

KI NO TSURAYUKI lived from 882 to 946. He is one of the major figures of Japanese literature, the author of the *Tosa Nikki*, the *Tosa Diary*, the principal editor of the *Kokin Shū* anthology, generally considered equal or superior to the first great collection, the *Manyōshū*, and the author of the preface to the *Kokin Shū*, which is the first masterpiece of Japanese prose. He was also one of the greatest Japanese calligraphers. He compiled another anthology — *Shinsen Shū*, "The New Collection of Poems," and a selection from the *Manyōshū*. Another reading for the second poem could be

> I do not know
> What they are thinking about
> In my birthplace, but
> I do know that
> The flowers still smell the same.

There is a reference to a famous quatrain by Wang Wei.

THE EMPEROR UDA reigned from 880 to 897. This poem is also attributed to Ki no Tsurayuki.

LADY UKON lived at the end of the ninth century. Nothing else is known of her.

ŌTOMO NO YAKAMOCHI lived from 718 to 785. He was the son of Ōtomo no Tabito, whose poems in praise of *sake* are famous, and who was a Grand Councillor of State. Yakamochi himself became a *Chūnagon*, Senior Councillor of State, after a career as a General, courtier, and provincial Governor. His family, which numbered several poets, was broken up after his death because of a crime of one of its members. His poetry is exceptional in the *Manyōshū* for its exquisite delicacy. He writes almost like a *précieux* of the eleventh century. The poem, "The frost lies white," is imitated from the many Chinese "dawn audience" poems. (Until its fall in 1912, it was the custom of the Chinese Court to open at dawn.) The Magpies' Bridge is both the bridge across the Milky Way by which the Herd Boy (Altair) visits the Weaving Girl (Vega) once a year on the seventh night of the seventh moon, and also a bridge in the Japanese Palace of those days, named, of course, after the mythical one. The poem can mean that he has very important business at court and has come early, or that he is stealing away from an assignation with one of the palace ladies, or that he has waited all night and she has not come. The orange blossoms were those of the *tachibana*, the small Japanese orange, probably not yet edible; the pearls were baroque abalone pearls.

THE EMPRESS YAMATOHIME was the wife of the Emperor Tenji, and after his death in 671 acted for a time as Regent.

ONAKATOMI NO YOSHINOBU lived in the latter part of the tenth century. He was a court official and one of the compilers of the Imperial Anthology, *Gosen Shū*. This is the first Japanese poem I ever translated; I was 15 years old. It is still one of my favorites.

THE EMPEROR YOZEI reigned from 877 to 884.

ARIWARA NO YUKIHIRA lived from 810 to 893. He was the elder brother of the famous Narihira. He became a State Councillor, *Chūnagon*.

Yukihira was sent into exile at Suma. As he crossed the mountains, he wrote this poem:

> The sudden chill of the autumn wind
> Penetrates the traveler's robe.
> The shore wind of Suma
> Blows through the pass.

From his exile he sent this poem:

> Tell those who ask for me
> That I am dragging water pails
> On the shore of Suma.

This means that he was working as a salt burner, which of course was not the case. However, he is supposed to have had two salt girl lovers, the sisters Matsukaze and Murasame. In the Noh play *Matsukaze*, they dance the famous dance, "the moon in the water pails," still often performed separately, and at the climax of the play, Matsukaze, whose name means "pine wind," dances to this poem, "the pine of Mount Inaba." *Inaba* also means "if I go away." *Matsu* can mean "long for" — that is — he puns "pine" and "pine." When Prince Genji was banished to Suma, the *Genji Monogatari* says, "Although the sea was some way off, yet when the melancholy autumn wind came blowing through the pass, the very wind of Yukihira's poem, the beating of the waves on the shore seemed very near." The dance which Matsukaze does to "the pine of Mount Inaba" is also the dance of the sky maiden in the Noh play *Hagoromo*, and this is, presumably, one of the sky maidens referred to in the poem by the Abbot Henjō; it is famous, too, for having been danced by one of the three fatal beauties of China, Yang Kuei Fei, for her lover, the Bright Emperor, Ming Huang, and it is still performed on the Moon Festival during the full moon of August. This is an example of the type of interlocking reference to be found in many Japanese as well as Chinese poems, and in this case could be prolonged indefinitely.

Matsukaze and Murasame are amongst the most popular Japanese dolls. Much of this note is in Waley's *Noh Plays*, which should be read by anyone interested in Japanese poetry.

THREE NAGA UTA OF HITOMARO:

I. Line 3: *Koto saegu* is a pillow word for Kara, "Korea," and means "chattering." This is one place where the pillow word is irrelevant. Later Kara came to mean China as well as Korea. In Hitomaro's day it is believed to have meant only the Southern Kingdom on the Korean Peninsula.

Line 6: *Miru* is *codium mucronatum*, a siphonale alga. The Chinese characters for the Japanese word read "deep-sea-pine." Many siphonales have a high protein content and are edible.

Line 8: "The jeweled sea tangle" is *tama mo oki tsu mo*, where *tama* is the Chinese character for "jade" or "jewel," which is possibly honorific, but may refer to the small floats like those on the sea grape. *Oki tsu mo* is "deep-sea weed," and could mean "kelp," which in modern Japanese is *konbu, Laminaria japonica.* It is impossible to say whether the line refers to two species or to one. These sea weed images echo poems in the *Nihonji.*

Line 15: "Tearing apart braided vines" probably echoes the Chinese cliché, "like separating dodder and buckwheat."

Line 21: *Ō bune no* is a pillow word for *watari,* which means "crossing over." Since it means "of great ships," it is practically impossible to fit it into the verse.

Line 27: *Tsuma gomoru,* "seclude wife," is really a pillow word for the *ya* of Mount Yakami, which happens to mean "house," and so—the hut erected especially for a newly married couple. In later Japanese, for instance, the modern *tanka* poetess Yosano Akiko, this pillow word with *yama* is best translated "honeymoon cottage in the mountains."

II. Line 11: *Isana tori* is a pillow word for *umi,* "sea," and means "whale catching"; it is even used of Lake Biwa, where there certainly have never been any whales. I understand the lines to mean that they used to walk seaward down the bay.

Line 15: *Ka ao,* "bright green," I think, justifies the translation, "jewelled." If so, *oki tsu mo* may mean a different plant.

Lines 17, 19: *Asa ha furu, yū ha furu:* "morning feather shake" "evening feather shake." Yakamochi uses *ha furu* for the quivering of a cuckoo's wings.

Line 25: *Tsuyu shimo no* is "like dew or hoarfrost," a pillow word for "leave," *oku (okite).*

Line 35: *Natsu kusa no,* "like grass in summer," is a pillow word for "wilt" or "languish," *naete.*

III. This is generally considered the greatest *naga uta* in the language.

Lines 1, 53: *Utsusemi* (modern Japanese, *utsushimi*) means the "body," the "mortal part," but, written with different Chinese characters (modern Japanese, still *utsusemi*), it also means the cast-off shell of an insect, a favorite image in Japanese for the transitoriness of life.

Line 7: The *tsuki* is *Zelkova keaki,* Sieb., or *Zelkova serrata,* Mak., the "Japanese elm," (*keaki* in Japanese). The reference, however, seems to me to be to the *wu t'ung* tree, *sterculia platanifolia* (*aogiri* in Japanese), the only tree in which the hōō, the Chinese *fêng-huang* or "phoenix," will breed or nest.

Lines 17-18: I believe this refers to mirage figures of the less extreme type, which come and go over barren fields. It may mean a fire seen over moorland.

Line 45: Ō *tori no*, "great bird," is a pillow word for Mount Hagai; it is applied to the hōō, swan, eagle, crane, etc. Presumably she was buried on Mount Hagai.

The *hanka* for these poems are given above.

The only *haiku* which needs any notes is the third by Bashō which describes a monk's retreat in the forest, so still that the only sound is the splash of a frog as the visitor approaches. "Summer grass where warriors dream" is paralleled by hundreds of Western poems from the Greek Anthology and the Bible to Carl Sandburg. It describes a battlefield.

The poems in the epigraph are from *The Tale of Genji* and are the pivot of the novel, the point at which the plot begins to flower into the profound world of Shingon Buddhist Tantrism which is the aspect of the novel which puts it in a class by itself, unquestionably the greatest as well as the philosophically wisest work of prose fiction in the world. The romaji is

> Koritoji ishi ma no mizu wa
> Yukinayami sora sumu tsuki
> No kagezo nagaruru
>
> Kakitsumete mukashi koi shiki
> Yuki moyo ni aware wo souru
> Oshi no uki neka

They are certainly Murasaki's best poems, and should be better known. Incidently, many of her poems, and others in this book are sung in the moving picture *The Tale of Genji*, which otherwise is very misleading, to say the least.

I am often asked the meaning of "Murasaki." Roughly it means "purple" or "purple dyed." Actually it is the name of the Lithospermum erythromrhizon, a purple rooted plant of the borage or forget-me-not family. A related species is called "puccoon" in the USA, and was once used as a rather fugitive dye.

BIBLIOGRAPHY

Japanese Odes, a translation of the Hyaku-nin-isshiu, by F. V. Dickins. Smith Elder and Co., London, 1866.

The Classical Poetry of the Japanese, by Basil Hall Chamberlain. Trübner and Co., London, 1880.

Genji Monogatari, translated by Suyematz Kenchio. Trübner and Co., London, 1882.

A History of Japanese Literature, by W. G. Aston. D. Appleton and Co., New York, 1889.

Persian and Japanese Literature (various translators), with an introduction by Richard J. H. Gottheil. The Colonial Press, London and New York, 1900.

Sword and Blossom Poems from the Japanese, translated by Shotaro Kimura and Charlotte M. A. Peake. T. Hasegawa, Tokio, 1901.

Primitive and Medieval Japanese Texts, translated by Frederick Victor Dickins. Clarendon Press, Oxford, 1906.

A Hundred Verses from Old Japan, a translation of the Hyakunin isshiu; by William N. Porter. The Clarendon Press, Oxford, 1909.

The Master Singers of Japan, translations from the Japanese poets by Clara A. Walsh. Wisdom of the East Series. John Murray, London, and E. P. Dutton and Co., New York, 1910.

A Year of Japanese Epigrams, translated by William N. Porter. Oxford University Press, London, 1911.

Japanese Poetry, by Basil Hall Chamberlain. John Murray, London, 1911.

Plays of Old Japan, the Noh, by Marie C. Stopes and Joji Sakurai. William Heinemann, London, 1913.

The Spirit of Japanese Poetry, by Yone Noguchi. Wisdom of the East Series. John Murray, London, and E. P. Dutton and Co., New York, 1914.

Imperial Japanese Poems of the Meiji Era, translated by Frank A. Lombard. Tokyo, 1915.

Japanese Lyrics, translated by Lafcadio Hearn. Houghton Mifflin Co., Boston, 1915.

"Noh", or Accomplishment, by Ernest Fenollosa and Ezra Pound. Alfred A. Knopf, Inc., New York, 1917. Very good.

Dreams from Japan and China, being transfusions from the Japanese and Chinese languages, by Gonnoské Komai. The Eastern Press, London, 1918.

Moons of Nippon, translations from poets of Old Japan, by Edna Worthley Underwood. Ralph Fletcher Seymour, Chicago, 1919.

Coloured Stars, versions of 50 Asiatic love poems, by Edward Powys Mathers. Houghton Mifflin Co., Boston, 1919.

Japanese Poetry, the "Uta", by Arthur Waley. The Clarendon Press, Oxford, 1919. Very good.

The Garden of Bright Waters, 120 Asiatic love poems, translated by Edward Powys Mathers. Houghton Mifflin Co., Boston, 1920. Good.

The No Plays of Japan, by Arthur Waley. George Allen and Unwin, Ltd., London, and Alfred A. Knopf, New York, 1921. Very good.

Early Japanese Poets, a translation of the Kokinshiu, by T. Wakameda. The Eastern Press, London, 1922.

Diaries of Court Ladies of Old Japan, translated by Annie Shepley Omori and Kochi Doi. Houghton Mifflin Co., Boston, 1923. Good.

Japanese Poetry, an historical essay, by Curtis Hidden Page. Houghton Mifflin Co., Boston, 1923.

Little Poems from Japanese Anthologies, translated by Evaleen Stein. M. Hopkinson, 1925.

Little Poems from the Japanese, translated by Laurence Binyon. The Swan Press, Leeds, 1925.

Tankas: Japanese Poems, by N. D. Horigoutchi, translated from the French version by L. K. Sparrow. London, 1925.

Japanese Classics, a book of reprints from transactions. Asiatic Society of Japan. Tokyo, 1925.

Leaving the Hermitage, by Rohan Koda, translated from the Japanese by Jiro Nagura. London, 1926.

Lotus and Chrysanthemum, an anthology of Chinese and Japanese Poetry, edited by Joseph Lewis French. Boni and Liveright, New York, 1927. Good.

Minyo, Folk-Songs of Japan, by Matsuhara. Shinseido, Tokyo, 1927.

Poetry of the Orient, an anthology edited by Eunice Tietjens. Alfred A. Knopf, New York, 1928. Good.

The Lady Who Loved Insects, translated by Arthur Waley. Blackmore, London, 1929. Good.

Early Japanese Poets: Complete translation of the Kokinshiu, by Wakameda. T. Yuhodo, Tokyo, 1929.

The Manyōsū, translated and annotated by Jan Pierson, Jr. Brill, Leiden, 1929-38. Very odd in places, but invaluable.

One Thousand Haiku, Ancient and Modern, translated by Asataro Miyamori. Dobunsha, Tokyo, 1930.

Japanese Scrapbook. Glenn Shaw. Hokuseido, Tokyo, 1932.

Anthology of Haiku, Ancient and Modern, translated and annotated by Asataro Miyamori. Maruzen, Tokyo, 1932. Fair, has texts, as have all his collections.

Nōgaku, Japanese Nō Plays, Beatrice Lane Suzuki. Wisdom of the East, Dutton, New York, 1932.

A Handful of Sand, translated from the works of Takuboku Ishikawa by Shio Sakanishi. Marshall Jones, Boston, 1934.

The Bamboo Broom; an Introduction to Japanese Haiku, translated by Harold Gould Henderson. Houghton Mifflin, Boston, 1934.

Four Nō Plays, M. Minakawa. Sekibundo, Tokyo, 1934.

Tangled Hair, translated by Shio Sakanishi from the work of Akiko Yosano. Marshall Jones, Boston, 1935. I have not seen this, she is a splendid modern tanka poet.

The Tale of Genji, in Six Parts, translated by Arthur Waley. Allen and Unwin, London, 1935. Very good. In print.

Naven, by Gregory Bateson. Cambridge University Press, Cambridge, 1936.

Masterpieces of Japanese Poetry, Ancient and Modern, translated and annotated by Asataro Miyamori. 2 vol. Maruzen, Tokyo, 1936. Fair, has texts.

Songs of a Cowherd, by Sachio Ito, translated by Shio Sakanishi. Marshall Jones, Boston.

An Anthology of Japanese Poems, translated by Asataro Miyamori. Maruzen, Tokyo, 1938. Fair, has texts.

Suye Mura, by John Fee Embree. Chicago University Press, Chicago, 1939. An excellent sociological study of a Japanese village.

Songs for Children Sung in Japan, by Yukuo Unyehara. Hokuseido, Tokyo, 1940.

The Manyōshu: One Thousand Poems Selected and Translated

from the Japanese. Nippon Gakujutsu Shinkokai. Iwanami, Tokyo, 1940.

The Manyōshū: One Thousand Poems Selected and Translated from the Japanese. University of Chicago Press, Chicago, 1941. Good, the same as the above.

Japanese Peasant Songs, compiled and annotated by John Fee Embree. American Folklore Society, Philadelphia, 1944.

Mei Kyoku Shu: Selected Songs. The Aloha Press, Honolulu Th., 1946.

A Pepper Pod: Classic Japanese Poems. Kenneth Yasuda. Alfred A. Knopf, New York, 1947.

Sword and Chrysanthemum, Ruth Benedict, still available as a pocket book, is propaganda by a person with very little knowledge of Japan, and extremely misleading. The best background for the poems in this book is Lady Murasaki's *The Tale of Genji* in the Waley translation. Stories of the samurai, for instance "The Forty-Seven Ronin", come from a period after most of the poems in this book were written. Pound's Noh translations, amongst his very greatest work, are now obtainable in *Collected Translations of Ezra Pound*, New Directions, New York City, 1953. Embree's *Suye Mura* is fine for the folk background. Readers of French should by all means read all of Bonneau's books.

Since the compilation of this bibliography Waley's *Uta* is brought back in print, by Lund Humphries, London, and his *Sei Shonagon* and *Noh Plays* by Grove Press, New York City. There are also new books by Kenneth Yasuda, R. H. Blyth, E. O. Reischauer, Donald Keene. Charles Eliot's *Japanese Buddhism* and the works of D. T. Suzuki are invaluable; both are now back in print.

PERIODICALS AND JOURNALS

"Basho and the Japanese Poetical Epigram", by Basil Hall Chamberlain. *Transactions of the Asiatic Society of Japan*, vol. 30, no. 2, pp. 243-362, 1902.

"The Japanese Man with the Hoe", by Paul Carus. *Open Court*, vol. 20, pp. 639 ff., 1906.

"The Literature of Primitive Japan", by Frederick Victor

Dickins. *Transactions and Proceedings of the Japan Society*, vol. 7, p. 354, 1907.

"The Makura-Kotoba of Primitive Japanese Verse", by Frederick Victor Dickins. *Transactions of the Asiatic Society of Japan*, vol. 35, part. 4, pp. 1-113, 1908.

"A Translation of the Japanese Anthology known as Hyakunin Isshiu", by Frederick Victor Dickins. *Journal of the Royal Asiatic Society*. pp. 357-391, 1909.

"The Plum in Japanese Poetry", by H. Saito. *Japan Magazine*, vol. I, pp. 103-107, 1910.

"Imperial Songs of Japan", translated by A. Lloyd. *Open Court*, vol. 25, pp. 532-539, 747-752, 1911.

"Japanese Poetry", by Yone Noguchi. *Transactions and Proceedings of the Japan Society*, Vol. 12, pp. 86-109, 1911.

"Translations from the No", by George Sansom. *Transactions of the Asiatic Society of Japan*, vol. 38, 3, pp. 175-176, 1911.

"The Literary Women of Japan and their work", by E. B. Mitford. *Book Monthly*, pp. 331-335, 1911.

"The Imperial Poetess of Japan", by J. Ingram Bryan. *Japan Magazine*, vol. 3, pp. 455-458, 1912.

"The Poet Laureate of Japan", by Arthur Lloyd. *Open Court*, vol. 26, pp. 694-698, 1912.

"The Kokinshu", by Ariel. *Japan Magazine*, vol. 3, pp. 614, 617, 713-14, 1912-1913.

"Songs of Japan", translated by Arthur Lloyd. *Open Court*, vol. 27, pp. 120-121; 121-123; 177-186, 1913.

"Songs the Geisha Sings", by Ingram J. Bryan. *Japan Magazine*, vol. 4, pp. 225-229, 1913-1914.

"The Manyoshu", by Ingram J. Bryan. *Japan Magazine*, vol. 4, pp. 293, 296, 1913-1914.

"Some Poems from the Manyōshū and Ryojin-hissho", by Arthur Waley. *Journal of the Royal Asiatic Society*, London, pp. 193-203, 1921.

"Appreciation of Nature in Japanese Poetry", by S. H. Wainright. *Transactions and Proceedings of the Asiatic Society of Japan*, vol. 2, pp. 36-54, 1925.

"Five Uta of Old Japan", by J. Caldwell-Johnston. *Asiatic Review*, vol. 22, pp. 639 ff. 1926.

"Japanese Classics", reprints. *Transactions of the Asiatic Society of Japan*, vol. I, pp. 165, 1926.

"Issa's Life and Poetry", by Max Bickerton. *Transactions of the Asiatic Society of Japan*, second series, vol. 9, pp. 111-154, 1932.

"Saikaku's 'Life of a Voluptuous Woman' Book Two", by Jan Rahder. *Acta Orientalia*, vol. 13, pp. 292-318, 1934. Rather odd, a great book in Japanese.

"The Cinematographic Principle and Japanese Culture", by Sergei Eisenstein. *Experimental Cinema* 8, Hollywood. No date. A little crazy; stimulating.

FOREIGN BOOKS AND ARTICLES

Geschichte der japanischen Literatur, by Karl Florenz. Amelangs, Leipzig, 1906.

"Poésies et anecdotes japonaises de l'époque des Taira et des Minamoto, suivies de l'histoire de ces 2 familles", by J. Dautremer. *Bibliothèque Orientale Elzévir*, vol. 86. E. Leroux, Paris, 1906.

Über japanische Dichtung, by Karl Florenz. Tägliche Rundschau, Beilage, 1906.

Joruri Gozen Junidanzoshi, by R. Kunze. Die Wahrheit, Tokyo, vol. 7, pp. 1-29, 1906.

Altjapanische Lyrik. Grenzboten, vol. 67, 1908.

"Japanische Lyrik aus 14 Jahrhunderten", by J. Kurth. *Die Fruchtschale*, vol. 17. R. Piper & Co., München, 1909.

Lieder der Liebe aus dem Reiche der aufgehenden Sonne, by L. Martin. Gartenlaube, 1909.

"Études sur le drame lyrique japonais (Nō)", by N. Peri. *Bulletin de l'École Française d'Extrême-Orient*, vol. 9, 11, 12, 13, 20. 1909-1920.

In Lust und Leid: Japanische Sagen und andere Dichtungen, by C. Eberhard. C. H. A. Kloss, Hamburg, 1910.

"Une Poétesse japonaise et son œuvre", by Takeshi Ishikawa. *Bulletin Société Franco-Japonaise*, No. 18, pp. 37-53, 1910.

Anthologie de la Littérature Japonaise des Origines au 20ᵉ siècle, by Michel Revon. Ch. Delagrave, Paris, 1910. It was translated into German.

"Der schöne Narihira", by O. Hauser. *Ton und Wort*, vol. 1, 1911.

Japanische Utas, by O. Hauser. A. Duncker, Berlin, 1911.
"La poésie japonaise", by J. Leclercq. *Bulletins de l'Académie Royale des Sciences, des Lettres, et des Beaux-arts de Belgique,* pp. 274-303. 1911.
Die japanische Lyrik, by H. Bethge. Hamburger Korrespondent, Beilage No. 6, 1912.
Etwas über altjapanische Lyrik, by E. V. Zenker. Die Wage, 1912.
"Liebesbrief", by H. Bethge. Nach einer unbekannten japanischen Dichterin. *Velhagen u. Klasings Monatshefte*, vol. 28, 1913.
"Japanische Lyrik", by Max Busing. *Geist des Ostens*, vol. 1, pp. 438-616, 1913-1914.
"La Poésie Japonaise et les Poèmes de la Libellule", by E. A. *Bulletin de la Société Franco-Japonaise de Paris*, pp. 17-23, 1914.
"Poèmes de la Libellule", by Judith Gautier. *Bulletin de la Société Franco-Japonaise de Paris*, pp. 25-55, 1914. Good.
"Trois chansons japonaises", by Léon Uhl. *Bulletin Société Franco-Japonaise*, pp. 77-78, 1918.
Die Geisha O-sen, by Klabund. Geisha-Lieder nach japanischen Motiven. München, 1918. Good.
Japanischer Frühling, by H. Bethge. Nachdichtungen japanischer Lyrik. Insel-Verlag, Leipzig, 1921.
"Cinq No Drames Lyriques japonais", traduits par N. Péri. *Classiques de l'Orient*, vol. 5. Bossard, Paris, 1921. Very good.
Tanabata: Das Sternenfest, by Kurt Meissner. O. Meissner, Hamburg. Redigiert von H. Bohner, 1923.
"Skizzen über japanische Lyrik", by O. Wolfgang. *Stimmen des Orients*, vol., 1, pp. 223-228, 1923.
Femmes japonaises et leur littérature, by Masaomi Yoshitomi. Henri Chariot, Paris, 1924.
Anthologie de la Littérature Japonaise Contemporaine, by M. Yoshitomi. Xavier Drevet, Grenoble, 1924. I have not seen.
"Das Tanabata-Fest", by Hyakuzo Kurata. *Das Junge Japan*, vol. 1, pp. 26-32, 60-63, 103-114, 149-153. 1924.
"Altjapanische Frauenlyrik," by E. v. Zenker. *Freie Welt*, vol. 4, pp. 13-20, no. 89; pp. 16-25, no. 90, 1924.
Wörterbuch zur altjapanischen Liedersammlung Koninshū, by K. Florenz. L. Friederichsen and Co., Hamburg, 1925.

"Poèmes du Vieux Japon", by Baronesse de Brimont. *Revue des Arts Asiatiques*, vol. 3, pp. 123-27, 1926.

"Der Shintoismus im japanischen Nō Drama", by Wilhelm Gundert. *Mittheilungen der Deutschen Gesellschaft für Natur- und Völkerkunde Ostasiens*, vol. 19, pp. 1-275, 1926.

"Liederreigen und Liebeswerben in Altjapan", by K. Florenz, *Orientalistische Literaturzeitung*, vol. 29, pp. 924-928, 1926.

"Choix de pièces du théâtre lyrique japonais", traduit par J. Penondeau. *Bulletin de l'École Française d'Extrême-Orient*, vol. 16, 27, 29, 31, 32, 1926-1932.

Contes d'amour de samouraïsū, xiiᵉ siècle japonais, traduit par Ken Sato. Sendhal et Compagnie, Paris, 1927.

"Die altjapanischen Jahrzeitpoesien aus dem Kokinshū", by Alexandre Canoch. *Asia Major*, vol. 4, pp. 240-389, 1927.

L'expression poétique dans le folklore japonais, traduit par Georges Bonneau. *Annales du Musée Guimet*, 42-44. Geuthner, Paris, 1933. Very good, as are all the Bonneau books which follow, all have texts.

Le moment poétique de Heian: Le Kokinshū I, par Georges Bonneau. Geuthner, Paris, 1933. Very good.

Die Langegedichte Yakamochi's aus der Manyōshū, by Eduard E. Florenz. Asia Major, Leipzig, 1933.

"Koshoku-Ichidai-Onna. Vie d'une amie de la volupté. Roman de mœurs paru en 1686 par Ibara Saikaku, traduit et annoté par Georges Bonmarchand. *Selbstverlag der Gesellschaft*, Tokyo, vol. 2, pp. 270-304, 1933. I have not seen. We need a good translation of Saikaku in English; I don't see how it could be complete in 34 pages.

Rythmes japonais, traduit par Georges Bonneau. Paul Geuthner, Paris, 1933. Very good.

La sensibilité japonaise, par Georges Bonneau. 3rd ed., L'auteur, Tokyo, 1934. Very good.

Le monument poétique de Heian: Le Kokinshū, II. Chefs-d'œuvres, par Georges Bonneau. Geuthner, Paris, 1934. Very good.

Anthologie de la poésie japonaise, traduit par Georges Bonneau. Geuthner, Paris, 1935. Very good.

Le Haiku, traduit par Georges Bonneau. Geuthner, Paris, 1935. Very good.

Lyrisme du temps présent, par Georges Bonneau. Geuthner, Paris, 1935. Very good, contains Yosano Akiko.

Une poétesse japonaise au xviie *siècle; Kaga no Tchiyo-jo,* par Gilberte Hla-Dorge. Maisonneuve, Paris, 1936.

"Haïkaï de Bashō et de ses disciples", traduit par E. Steinilber-Oberlin et Kuni Matsuo. *Collection japonaise, Institut International de Coopération Intellectuelle.* Institut, Paris, 1926. Good.

Les haïkaï de Kikakou, textes et commentaires japonais traduits pour la première fois, par E. Steinilber-Oberlin et Kuni Matsuo. Crès, Paris, 1937. Good.

Le problème de la poésie japonaise. Technique et traduction, par Georges Bonneau. Geuthner, Paris, 1938. Good.